The Little Book of

MORE
ABUSE

D0319310

The Little Book of

MORE ABUSE

More one-liners for the really
annoying people in your life

JASMINE BIRTLES

BXTREE

First published 2002 by Boxtree
an imprint of Pan Macmillan Ltd
Pan Macmillan, 20 New Wharf Road, London N1 9RR
Basingstoke and Oxford
Associated companies throughout the world
www.panmacmillan.com

ISBN 0 7522 1498 5

Copyright © 2002 Jasmine Birtles

The right of Jasmine Birtles to be identified as the author
of this work has been asserted by her in accordance with the
Copyright, Designs and Patents Act 1988.

9 8 7 6 5

A CIP catalogue record for this book is available from
the British Library.

Designed by seagulls
Printed and bound in Great Britain
by CPI Bath

INTRO

Well, I'm glad to see you've got brains enough to buy this second instalment of the coolest insults in the world. Because, hey, a bit of nastiness costs nothing, right? . . . Well, apart from the price of this book, obviously, I'm not stupid! Remember to do your bit wherever you are. If you think she's got a face to launch a thousand dredgers, tell her. If you think he's got a room-temperature IQ and is dumber than a box of hair – lay it on him. Do your duty – tell it as it is and make sure that if you've said anything to offend it's purely intentional. Go on – spread a little unhappiness.

What is this?
Be Nice to Freaks Week?

There you go again.
Mistaking me for someone
who gives a toss.

Don't try me.
I'm pre-menstrual.
I could kill you now and
get off with a caution.

Oh, go and play in the traffic.

Nice outfit. Go stand
on a street corner, you
could make some money.

9

Your face – my arse.

Look at her. One more facelift
and she'll have a beard.

Interesting clothes. You're
wearing them for a bet, right?

Sorry, I like my men a little
higher up the food chain.

Here's 10p. Go call
someone who cares.

Any part of you that touches
me you're not getting back.

Upset? Me? No! I just thought
your BMW would look better
with half a gallon of acid
poured over it.

He's currently in training
for 'The Most Annoying
Man in Britain Award'
and I think he'll win.

If I'm from Venus and
you're from Mars, what's
that in Uranus?

Next time you cross
the road, don't look.

It's so sad, he spent all
that time washing and
combing his hair and then
forgot to bring it with him.

16

Of course you're special.
You went to a special
school, right?

Kiss you? But I haven't
been inoculated yet.

If you can't live
without me, how come
you're not dead yet?

Oh, murder's such a horrid word. I prefer to call it assisted suicide.

You've got an idea!
Yes, I heard. But it died
of loneliness, didn't it?

You, George W. Bush and Dan Quayle – in a stupid contest who'd win?

Why don't you just cut your
losses and join a freak show?

When he comes into a room
the mice jump on chairs.

He's the kind you have to
look at twice – the first
time you don't believe it.

She loves nature, in spite
of what it did to her.

How did you get here?
Did someone leave
your cage open.

I bet your mum
has a loud bark.

I tell you what to do
and you do it. Round here
that's called teamwork.

I like you. You're such
a screw-up you make
me look successful.

Uh-oh, a couple of
clowns short of the full
circus, aren't we?

Some call it blackmail
but I like to think of it as
redistribution of wealth.

With friends like you,
who needs enemas?

Which part of the phrase
'piss off' do you not
understand?

29

Mm, I'd like to help but
in this shop the only thing
that would fit your size is
the cubicle curtain.

I'd like to help you out.
Which way did you come in?

I'm busy now. Can I ignore
you some other time?

So a thought crossed your mind? Must have been a lonely journey.

Some day you'll find yourself
– and wish you hadn't.

Who picks your clothes?
Stevie Wonder?

D'you know, in poor light,
without my glasses and after
a bottle of vodka you could
almost pass for attractive.

No, really, I'm glad
you've found someone. After
all, if someone wants to go out
with *you* it shows anything
is possible.

Your team would follow
you anywhere – but only
out of curiosity.

36

Well, there are so many
nice people in the world I
just want to balance it out.

No, it's a crap picture,
you can't draw, and I don't
care if you are three.

Ugly? She got done for
indecent exposure and only
her face was showing.

I'm glad to be out with you.
I'm at that age when I look
forward to a dull evening.

I can't be angry with
you today – it's 'Be Kind
to Animals' week.

Use your head – it's the
little things that count.

I hear the only place you're
ever invited is outside.

So you were born on a farm.
Any more in the litter?

I know you're nobody's
fool but perhaps someone
will adopt you.

Don't bother turning the other cheek – it's just as ugly.

Him a singer?
He couldn't carry a tune
in an armoured car.

He's nobody's fool –
he's a freelancer.

You remind me of a
toothache I once had.

With the right amount
of training you could get
to be a nobody.

He never opens his mouth
unless he has nothing to say.

If your IQ were any lower
you'd be a privet hedge.

He's on everybody's lips –
like a cold sore.

I love your red dress, it
matches your eyes.

She's so ugly, five peeping
Toms have topped themselves.

If brevity is the soul of wit,
your willy must be a riot.

She's one tit short
of the full udder.

He was fat and ugly
before he went on a diet.
Now he's thin and ugly.

He tried to get a job as an
idiot but was underqualified.

You're the kind of person
who can say absolutely
nothing – and mean it.

What he lacks in intelligence
he makes up for in stupidity.

With a face like that you
couldn't pull a chain!

He's like a son to me –
insolent, ungrateful,
disrespectful . . .

He started at the
bottom and sank.

He has no equals –
only superiors.

Don't leave me. I want to
forget you exactly as you are.

Are you trying to get fit
or just having one?

Don't go outside – people
will think it's Hallowe'en.

You'll lose your looks when
you're older – if you're lucky.

He's like an oil well;
always boring.

So you've changed your
mind. Does the new one
work any better?

Nice dress. What make is it?
Clearance?

I thought men like
that shot themselves.

Of course I like children,
especially on toast.

You couldn't fart and chew
gum at the same time.

If you were a building
you'd be condemned.

Nice mouth.
When does it shut?

I don't know what makes you
so stupid, but it really works.

Please close your mouth so
I can see the rest of your face.

If your IQ were any
lower you'd trip over it.

She's turned many a head in
her day – and a few stomachs.

He's a prime candidate
for natural deselection.

He donated his body to
science before he was
finished with it.

The gates are down, the
lights are flashing but the
train ain't coming.

Yes, you're over eighteen
but your IQ isn't.

You're as much use
as a condom machine
in the Vatican.

What is this? A meeting
of the ugly convention?

You call that dancing?
I've seen people on
fire move better.

I know you like me,
I can see your tail wagging.

She got into the
gene pool while the
lifeguard wasn't watching.

He's got an IQ of 2
and it takes 3 to grunt.

He has two brains –
one's lost and the
other's out looking for it.

If brains were taxed
she'd get a rebate.

70

You're proof that
evolution can go in reverse.

The wheel's spinning
but the hamster's dead.

His nose is so big he
can smell the future.

If you gave her a penny for
her thoughts you'd get change.

72

Do you want people to accept you as you are or do you want them to like you?

Do you still have a terrible empty feeling – in your skull?

73

Do you need a
licence to be that ugly?

I'd like to see things
from your point of view,
but I can't seem to get my
head that far up my arse.

If you had another
brain cell it would be lonely.

He's not drunk, exactly,
he just fell off the floor.

I may look like I'm doing
nothing, but at a cellular
level I'm really very busy.

76

I don't work here. I'm a consultant. Consultants don't work, they just get paid.

Look, in this organization
the chain of command
goes: amoeba, toilet
brush, then you.

At least I have a
positive attitude about
my destructive habits.

I'm working on the principle that the only way to reduce violence is to kill everybody.

Try not to have any
ideas – they only lead
to complications.

If you ever become a mother,
can I have one of the calves?

If you stand close enough
to his ear you can
hear the ocean.

If he were a tomcat
you'd have him done.

So it's lasagne, is it?
I thought you'd just
thrown up on the plate.

Attractive? She wouldn't
even make Crufts.

Is that a new aftershave
you're wearing or have I
just stepped in something?

I wish I'd known you
when you were alive.

You're about as useful
as a chocolate fireguard.

Her face bears the imprint of
the last man who sat on it.

I've got two words for you –
Thera Pee.

Oh, I'm sorry, I dozed off –
did you finally say
something interesting?

Thanks for the drink, it'll help
me forget my troubles . . .
Nope, you're still there.

Oh no, look at you! Anyone else hurt in the accident?

The last time I saw a body like that it was being milked.

Why grow on your face what
grows naturally on your bum?

You've got the charisma of a
knitting pattern.

You've got a body to die for – and a face to protect it.

With my brains and your body we would make one very smart walrus.

Do you always talk this much or are you breaking in a new tongue?

I'd ask you to count to
ten and calm down, but I
know that's six more than
your personal best . . .

Look, here's 50p – go and buy
yourself a new wardrobe.

I hear you've been
on a self-improvement
course. Bet they didn't
know where to start, eh?

Normally I never kiss
on a first date, but in your
case let's not talk either.

I haven't laughed this much
since I noticed your shirt.

I hope you live to be
as old as your jokes.

If I had a face like yours
I'd teach my arse to smile.

Please turn off your mouth.
It's still running.

His voice is even
louder than his tie.

You've given me something
to live for – revenge.

If I've said anything to
insult you it's not for want
of trying, believe me.

He's so short, when it rains
he's the last one to know.

You must be older than you look. No one could get that stupid so fast.

Why don't you go home
and tell your mother
she wants you?

Just because you smell
like an ape it doesn't
mean you're Tarzan.

When your IQ
reaches 50 – sell.

I can't believe the sperm that
created you beat twenty
million others.

It must be a thrill for you
to know someone who
wears underwear.

Have you got a minute?
Tell me everything you know.

He's a man of few words –
but not few enough.

Can I borrow your face
for a couple of days?
My arse is going on holiday.

Use your brain. It's the
little things that count.

Go on, I know you like me –
I can see your tail wagging.

He's so ugly they've printed
his face on airline sick bags.

Excuse me, haven't
I seen you in the movies.
You served me popcorn, right?

I'm like his proctologist – I've seen enough of that arsehole.

Look at him – the pin-up boy for vasectomies.

So do you come here often,
or has there been a
breakout at the zoo?

You'd think such a
little mind would be lonely
in such a big head.

I wouldn't say you're fat but you're two of the biggest hippos I ever saw.

I think you've been working
with glue too much.

You can park a bus in the
shadow of his arse.

Sure you've got animal
magnetism – only animals
want to be near you.

Yeah, I could sleep with you.
After all, beauty is just
a light switch away.

What happened to your face?
Do you step on rakes for fun?

I don't think you're an
idiot, but then what's
my opinion compared to
thousands of others?

He's as bald
as a badger's arse.

I've seen wounds better
dressed than her.

You'd forget your bollocks if
you didn't keep them in a bag.

Last time I saw a mouth like
that it had a hook in it.

Ooh, you'll be doing
joined-up writing next.

She's like the Venus de Milo –
pretty but not all there.

If you went to a mind-reader
they wouldn't bother charging.

If my dog was as ugly as you
I'd shave his arse and make
him walk backwards.

He's the definition of
dark and handsome.
When it's dark, he's
handsome.

I'll buy you a beer if you'll
drink somewhere else.

Why don't you put your
nose in your ear and
blow your brains out?

What holds your ears apart?

If sex appeal were dynamite
you couldn't blow the cobwebs
off your own balls.

Being a bitch gives
me more satisfaction
than you do, honey.

Go make friends
with your own species.

I don't mind you talking
so long as you don't
mind me not listening.

If I promise to miss you,
will you go away?

I'm blonde.
What's your excuse?

BIOG

Jasmine Birtles is an Inter-Galactic Thrombal warrior from Scrotal Planet 5. She is made entirely from titanium and nougat offcuts and cannot stand in the rain for long without going soggy. She has travelled to Earth as part of her mission to promote her bestselling video, *Space Aliens Toned My Stomach In Just Thirty Days*. Should this mission fail, her second directive is to destroy the cultural life of Croydon – except that someone's already done that. On an earlier mission to Earth she ran her own carbon-dating agency, for people who were looking for someone with the right chemistry. She could find your ideal match in moments, give or take a million years' age difference. A recent runner-up in the Miss Exoskeleton pageant (Crustacean Section), she told judges that she loves wiring and cables, although not on a first date. Her favourite food is tarmac.